# SHORES, REEFS, AND THE DEEP

written by Christina Wilsdon
reviewed by Robert E. Budliger

Reader's Digest
Children's Books®

Pleasantville, New York • Montreal, Québec • Bath, United Kingdom

# Sea and Shore

Where ocean and land meet is called the **coast**. The seas, bays, gulfs, and other parts of the ocean that poke into the land also have coasts. All these coasts add up to about 372,000 miles. That is enough coastline to wrap around Earth's middle at the equator nearly 15 times.

Coasts are filled with living things. Many sea creatures live on coastal shores. Some live in the zone that is washed by waves. Some live just beyond the water's reach. Other animals live offshore. Colorful coral reefs in warmer waters are home to many of these animals.

Some animals, however, live about as far from the coast as they possibly can. These animals live in the deepest parts of the ocean, where it is dark and cold. Some live on the ocean's floor and in the deepest places that humans have ever explored.

## Did You Know?

Earth, the moon, and the sun all have gravity, an invisible force that makes these objects pull on one another. The moon and sun's gravity also tugs on Earth's water. This changes the level of the ocean's water in most parts of the world four times a day. When the water level rises on a beach, it is called high **tide**. When the water drops away from shore, it is called low tide.

## What's That Word?

As you read, you will see words that are in **bold** type. Look for them in the glossary on page 22 to learn what they mean.

## Big Blue Marble

From outer space, Earth looks like a swirly big blue marble. The blue is the ocean, which covers almost three-quarters of Earth's surface. The land separates the world ocean into five smaller ones: the Pacific, the Atlantic, the Indian, the Southern, and the Arctic.

*Stranded whales are a sad sight on a shoreline. Rescuers keep these pilot whales wet until they are returned to a safe place in the open sea.*

# Beach Life

Animals that live on seashores full-time face challenges that most ocean animals do not. The motion of waves is one challenge. Some animals are regularly pounded by powerful waves. They are tugged by the surf as it slides down the shore.

Animals such as barnacles avoid being washed away by gluing themselves to rocks. A mussel, which lives inside a two-part shell, hangs on to rocks with tough threads made by its body.

Other animals survive by burying themselves. Clams burrow into mud and sand. Then they stick up a long body part called a siphon to reach the water above. Their bodies take in oxygen from the water and filter out meals of tiny living things called **plankton**.

## I'll Have the Oysters

It should be easy to figure out what oystercatchers eat! These shorebirds have strong bills for jabbing into oyster shells. They also use their bills to pry snails off rocks.

## Poking Around

Beach creatures must also be on guard against **predators,** such as birds that visit seashores to feed. Shorebirds have thin bills for poking into sand and mud, picking at seaweed, or pecking up tidbits from the water. Some of them have long legs for wading in water. The shore offers them a feast of insects, worms, crabs, clams, and other tiny creatures to eat.

Laughing Gull

*It may mean flying hundreds of miles, but a gannet returns to the same place every year to nest.*

There is also the problem of not enough water! When the tide goes out, animals farther up the shore lose the protection of water. But they have ways to avoid drying up. A barnacle closes its shell tightly. Mussels live in clumps, which helps cut down on how much water they lose while the tide's out.

# Tide Pool Life

When it drops down the beach at low tide, the ocean leaves behind puddles onshore. Puddles form in dips on mud flats or sandy shores. They form in basins among piles of rocks. These puddles are called **tide pools.** They can be as small as a cereal bowl or as big as a rowboat.

A tide pool is filled with life. Sea stars cling to rocks. Little crabs hide under the rocks. Bright green anemones spangle the pool like flowers. Tiny snails make wriggly trails in the sand.

Ocean animals live in a **habitat** where the temperature does not change quickly. Levels of oxygen and salt in the water change slowly, too. But they can all change in just a few hours in a tide pool. A small tide pool can heat up quickly in the sun. Its oxygen level then drops.

Animals in the tide pool live through these changes until the tide rolls in again. Anemones pull in their **tentacles.** Crabs burrow into damp seaweed. Many tide pool animals feed on plankton delivered by the ocean. Crabs eat seaweed and dead fish. Some tide pool animals eat each other.

## A Salty Story

A tide pool's water **evaporates,** which means it turns into a gas and goes into the air. The tide pool starts drying up just like a puddle on a sidewalk. This makes the pool more salty, because there is less and less water to hold the same amount of salt.

A tide pool looks as if it would be a safe, cozy place to live in. But a tide pool also presents challenges for animals living in it—ones that ocean animals don't face.

## Star Bright

A sea star eats other animals. It can open a clam by clasping it with its arms and steadily pulling on the shell. As soon as a gap opens, the sea star's stomach bulges out of its body. It covers the clam's body and digests it. Then the stomach slips back into the sea star's body.

# Shore Leave

Some animals are most at home in the water, but they need to use the shore for parts of their lives.

Sea turtles live in the ocean, but they are all born on land. Female sea turtles drag themselves up on beaches to lay eggs in the sand. They head right back into the ocean when this job is done. The babies also dash toward the ocean as soon as they hatch.

The green sea turtle starts life as an egg that looks like a Ping-Pong ball. The hatchling that pops out of the egg is about 2 inches long. The baby sea turtle drifts with the waves at first, feeding on tiny animals. It spends a few years at sea growing up. As an adult, it eats only plants and **algae.**

A female green sea turtle may spend 20 years in the ocean before coming back to the beach where she hatched. Then she will climb ashore there to lay her own eggs.

## Fish Out of Water

Some fish come ashore from time to time. Fish called grunions wriggle ashore on parts of Southern California's coast during an extra-high tide. They lay their eggs in the sand. Then the surf sweeps the grunions back into the ocean. When another extra-high tide sweeps up the beach two weeks later, the eggs are ready to hatch.

## Did You Know?

Seals also come ashore to give birth. Harp seals gather in large herds on icy shores in the early spring to have their pups. The seal pups stay on land, drinking their mothers' rich milk. Pups drink milk until they are about two weeks old. By the time a pup is about a month old, it has shed its baby fur. It starts to swim and eat fish in the water. On land, its main predators are polar bears and people. Now it must beware of sharks and killer whales, too.

*Sea turtles like this loggerhead are in danger because so many people are building on their nesting places.*

# What Is a Coral Reef?

Colorful coral reefs are just offshore in warm tropical seas. A coral reef looks like a beautiful flower garden. But no plants grow there. The bright colors and strange shapes belong to animals. They share a habitat that has been built over many years by tiny soft-bodied animals called **coral polyps.**

Coral polyps are related to jellyfish. A single coral polyp is like a small squishy tube. It has a mouth but no brain. Stinging tentacles wave around the mouth. A polyp uses its tentacles to catch plankton to eat.

Coral polyps that build reefs live in large groups called colonies. Each polyp makes a hard tube and lives inside it. This tube is called its skeleton. The polyp also makes a kind of skin that goes over the outside of its skeleton. This skin joins up with the skins of the polyps around it.

Tiny plantlike living things called algae live inside many kinds of corals. They often give the coral its color. A coral reef grows over time because the polyps' skeletons remain in place after the polyps die. New polyps build on top of these old skeletons. The reef grows larger and larger. It may start to look like an underwater forest of strangely shaped trees.

## Dirty Fish?

Fish live in water, so you'd think they are always clean. Not so! Fish suffer from pests called parasites. Parasites may suck blood and weaken a fish. So little fish called cleaner wrasses keep other fish clean. They eat the parasites and also nibble off any flecks of dead skin. The wrasses get a meal, and the bigger fish gets a good scrubbing.

# Reef Life

Stripes, spots, colors, dots—coral reef fish dazzle the eye! A reef may include as many as 150 kinds of coral! By day, the reef is a riot of color as fish swim about, searching for food. Their bright colors help them find mates, too.

At night, while many colorful fish lie low, other reef animals get busy. Squid and octopuses creep out of cracks in the reef. Sea urchins, sea stars, and crabs crawl about in search of food.

Animals called sponges don't need to leave home to look for food. A sponge simply filters plankton from water flowing through tiny holes in its surface. Tiny fuzzy cells inside its body help keep the water moving through it. Sea slugs, sea stars, and even turtles feed on sponges. Hermit crabs and shrimp sometimes live inside them.

Parrotfish feed directly on the corals' skeletons. A parrotfish's strong teeth can scrape algae off coral, but it comes with some stony skeleton. The parrotfish digests the algae, and any bits of skeleton pass out of its body in its droppings.

## Room to Rent

A coral reef can be a crowded place. Finding a place to live isn't always easy. Some sponges, like these, solve this problem by making a poison that kills coral polyps. This sure helps them clear a place for themselves!

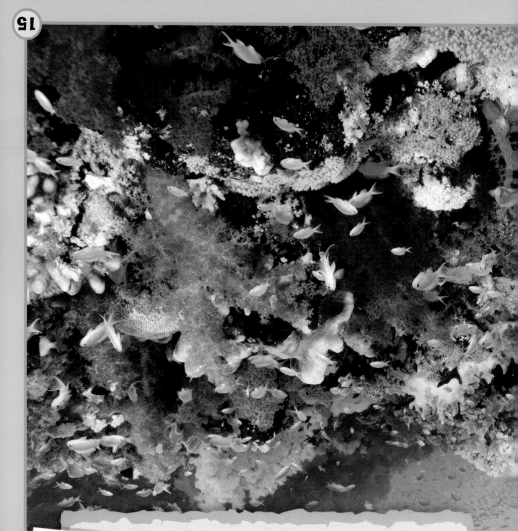

## Ouch!

Lionfish have spines in their fins that are loaded with venom. The fish uses this venom to defend itself against predators. It doesn't need venom to catch fish to eat—it just snaps them up!

# Hunters of the Reef

Many reef animals are predators. Cone snails sting fish, worms, and other snails. Other snails eat polyps, clams, sea stars, and sea urchins. Sea slugs eat sponges and anemones. Pistol shrimp snap their claws to shoot down fish with "shock waves"—sharp bursts of pressure like underwater cracks of thunder.

The biggest predators of the reef are sharks. Whitetip, blacktip, and gray reef sharks are familiar sights in many Pacific Ocean coral reefs and some Indian Ocean reefs. Whitetip sharks often spend the day lolling in underwater caves in groups. At night, they come out to eat octopuses, crabs, lobsters, shrimp, and fish. Blacktip reef sharks also eat fish, octopuses, lobsters, and shrimp.

Blind sharks live on coral reefs along parts of Australia's coast. There they feed on anemones, shrimp, crabs, and cuttlefish. A blind shark can see just fine. Its name comes from its habit of shutting its eyes when it is lifted out of the water.

## In Plain Sight

Wobbegongs are wide, flat sharks that live near Australia. They are covered with spots and splotches, which help them blend in with coral. When fish come close...*chomp!*

Gray reef sharks tend to swim along the outside of coral reefs near the seafloor. They swim long distances as they hunt for food.

## Beware!

Moray eels hide in cracks and holes in a reef. When a fish swims by, a moray lunges out to grab it with sharp teeth. Moray eels can even eat big meals such as squid and large fish. A moray has a second set of jaws in its throat that helps to swallow its super-sized servings.

# What's in the Deep?

Far from shore, out past the coral reefs, are the ocean's wide-open spaces. Different kinds of animals live at different levels in this vast area.

Some of the animals live in a twilight zone. They light up the gloom by glowing. Ax-shaped hatchetfish have rows of lights on their bellies. Bristlemouths and little lanternfish are speckled with miniature lights on their stomachs and sides. These lights help the fish blend in with the little bit of sunlight that glows faintly in the water above them. It hides them from hungry fish below.

Glowing also helps fish lure **prey**. The dragonfish has a glowing whisker on its chin that attracts other fish, putting them in easy reach of its toothy jaws. Having lights also helps fish find mates. The pattern of lights helps them identify other fish of the same species.

Giant squid, sperm whales, and frill sharks also dwell in the twilight zone. A giant squid can grow to be about 60 feet long!

# Did You Know?

Some fish and other animals make light when oxygen mixes with chemicals stored in parts of their bodies. Fireflies produce their own light this way. Other animals, including some fish, glow because their bodies hold pockets of small living things that actually produce the light.

## Glowers

Dragonfish

Lanternfish

Hatchetfish

A sperm whale feasts on squid and octopuses. A sperm whale can dive as deep as 2 miles, and it can stay underwater for more than an hour! That gives it plenty of time for a long struggle.

# Mysteries of the Deep

The ocean's dark zone is far beyond the reach of sunlight. Animals living there dwell in cold and total darkness. Without light, no plants can grow. As a result, there isn't a lot to eat in the dark zone.

Many deep-sea animals depend on bits of dead plants, animals, and one-celled living things trickling down from above. Sometimes, a feast arrives in the form of a whole dead whale!

Deep-sea fish have ways of getting enough to eat, too. Gulper eels have gigantic mouths. They lure prey closer with a flashing light on the tip of their long tail. Then they take in their prey with huge jaws. The eel's body can stretch to fit a fish as big as it is. An anglerfish, however, can eat fish *twice* its size.

Viperfish often move up into the twilight zone to feed at night. Most viperfish have lights along their bodies. Their teeth are long and sharp. A viperfish's stomach is coated with a dark lining so that any glow-in-the-dark meals it eats won't make the predator shine, too!

## Deep, Secret Places

Deep in the ocean are places where hot water pours from cracks in the ocean floor. Bacteria living here can turn minerals in the water into food. Other animals such as crabs, shrimp, and snails live here, too. Some of them eat the bacteria. Giant tube worms have bacteria living inside them that help keep them fed.

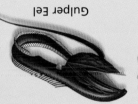

Gulper
Shark

## Deep-sea Swimmers

Viperfish

Crossed-toothed
Perch

Gulper Eel

## How Deep?

The deepest place on Earth may be the Marianas Trench. This trench is nearly 7 miles beneath the ocean's surface. Scientists explored it in a deep-sea **submersible**. Even at that depth, they saw anemones and other living things.

# Glossary

**algae:** Plantlike living things that use sun, air, and water to make food

**coast:** A place where the ocean meets land

**coral polyp:** A soft-bodied animal with a tube-shaped skeleton

**evaporate:** To turn from a liquid into a gas

**habitat:** The environment in which a plant or animal lives

**plankton:** Tiny living things that float mainly in the ocean's upper layers

**predator:** An animal that eats other animals

**prey:** Animals that are eaten by other animals

**submersible:** A strong metal craft used to explore the depths of the ocean

**tentacles:** Long flexible organs around an animal's mouth or head that help it move, grasp, and feel

**tide pool:** A puddle left behind on a shore when the tide goes out

**tides:** The regular rise and fall of the ocean along coasts